SAYING THE RIGHT THING
WHEN YOU DON'T KNOW WHAT TO SAY

This book will help you magnify the love you express for others by ten-fold. You'll learn effective communication techniques for engaging with those who are suffering. *Saying The Right Thing* is a beautiful compilation of wisdom from Paula Shaw that will no doubt shine an abundance of healing into a world that desperately needs it.

—Ryan McCormick, host & producer, "The Outer Limits of Inner Truth"

Shaw gives a stunningly fresh perspective on a very old topic—grief, loss, what to say, what not to say. A deeply moving and inspirational look at just exactly how to be more effective at the greatest time of loss. The author gives you tangible direction and tools to fully prepare you to bring so much more than the cliché ineffective tracks of the past 100 years! A very good read. I read the whole book in one night!

—Donald Samuel Meredith, author, *The DST Revolution*

[This book] gives me the words and the actions that help me to not only show up confidently for those I care about, but to also truly be able to help them when they are struggling and need a friend.

—Sophia Alsadek, engineer

Paula tackles some of the TOUGH issues that we face, but often don't talk about. Rather than giving you a "script" for the right thing to say, she actually teaches you how to listen and understand. Then she gives you real, simple, practical suggestions for how to engage in a conversation that leaves the other person feeling heard and validated.

—Amy Mewborn, CEO, author, operations and strategy expert

Saying the Right Thing is just what this broken world needs! People who don't want to deal with this "touchy-feely" part of life are exactly the ones who will benefit from Paula's years of education and experience distilled into this powerful, compact book

—Brenda Meredith, manager, program controls, General Dynamics NASSCO

My boss's husband was dying, and we had to work together every day. I was at a total loss as to whether or not to bring it up. I wanted to help her in any way I could but not knowing what to say…I just stayed silent. Then I read *Saying the Right Thing*. The very next day I approached her with love and confidence. She wept in my arms and thanked me. From that day on we walked through his dying process together. Thank you, Paula.

—Amy Wynne, interior design

An unexpected tragedy in the life of a friend put me in the horribly awkward position of wanting to support her but having absolutely no idea what to say in the face of such a terrible loss. Saying the Right Thing gave me the answers I needed to not only show up but to actually be of help to her.

—Katherine Foster, fundraiser

SAYING THE RIGHT THING
WHEN YOU DON'T KNOW WHAT TO SAY

PAULA SHAW   CADC, DCEP

Wisdom
Editions
Minneapolis

Wisdom
Editions
Minneapolis

FIRST EDITION SEPTEMBER 2018
SAYING THE RIGHT THING, Copyright © 2018 by Paula Shaw.
All rights reserved.

Printed in the United States of America.
10 9 8 7 6 5 4 3 2 1

Cover and interior design: Gary Lindberg

ISBN: 978-1-7327944-1-2

SAYING THE RIGHT THING

RIGHT THING

WHEN YOU DON'T
KNOW WHAT TO SAY

PAULA SHAW   CADC, DCEP

TABLE OF CONTENTS

INTRODUCTION

Over my twenty-seven years of counseling people in emotional pain, I have been asked hundreds of times, "What do I say to someone who has just lost a child, or a husband, or a job? I'm afraid to call because I don't know the right thing to say, or how to help and not hurt."

Is this human dilemma familiar to you? Have you been there? Have you been the injured party or the avoidant party, afraid to make the call and say the wrong thing? I think we have all been on both sides at one time or another, and it's a really tough place to be. We want to help and support, but we truly don't know which words might bring comfort and which words might cause pain.

And lately, a new concern has emerged among men who are terrified by this new movement of women who are bold and unafraid to speak their truths. They are calling bullshit on inappropriate behavior from men. They are identifying certain words and behaviors that used to be known as "flirting" but are now considered to be harassment. Men are scared, confused and somewhat baffled about what is OK and what is not.

While I believe this is something that has been long overdue, I also have a heart for men who have been raised with a certain standard of behavior who are now being told that this standard is deeply flawed. They were brought up to think "flirting" was OK, even desired by women. What they thought was OK is now "No Way" for a lot of women.

I actually had a man at the radio station where I do my show say to me one day, "I love that outfit you are wearing." Then, as a flushed look of concern came over his face, he said, "Is that OK to say?" He was genuinely worried that he might be objectifying me or sexualizing me by simply complimenting what I was wearing. To ease his angst, I joked, "As long as you're not pinching my butt as you say it!"

The bottom line is that there has never been a time when what we say matters more. Our words, which have always had power, are now more powerful than ever.

Over the years in my practice I have been constantly amazed by the power of words spoken and also by the power of words unspoken. The emotional pain that can be caused by both is staggering and is actually the root of most relationship distress.

Today, more than ever, people are agonizing over not knowing the right thing to say. I want to relieve that angst by giving you specific words and actions that are effective and helpful. I will also tell you those to avoid like the plague because they are damaging and hurtful.

This is not a book about theory… it's a "go to" for specifics. I am tired of seeing people in my office who either weren't helped because of other's fears, or who didn't offer help themselves because of their own fears. "Time is up," as Oprah so appropriately said it. We have to stop hiding behind our fear. It is time to speak up when someone needs to hear your words. My desire is to help you feel confident about your ability to do so effectively.

It's time to open up this conversation, because this dilemma is ubiquitous. I don't know about you, but they didn't offer Saying the Right Thing 101 at my high school. There was no training except what we experienced growing up, and too often that was dysfunctional or abusive, and that is not what we want to pass on. We need a way to up-level our support and communication skills so we can be confident that our conversations with others are helpful and not patronizing or abusive.

My goal in this book is to give you sound, effective, proven answers to those very real issues.

Before we examine what is truly helpful, let's take a look at why we so often say and do the wrong things.

WHY DON'T WE KNOW WHAT TO SAY?

Our culture has this very archaic idea that if an experience is ubiquitous and part of normal life, we should automatically know how to navigate it. So if we do the math, it adds up like this. Everyone loves someone. Everyone experiences emotional pain at some time or another. Since this experience is common, then of course it follows that everyone should naturally have skills that would enable him or her to comfort and support a hurting person they love. This would probably be true if our social and familial experiences hadn't messed with the perfect creatures we were upon arrival.

The unfortunate flaw in the above formula is that we all come to every situation with a myriad of unique experiences that may or may not prepare us to be effective helpers.

For example, if you grew up in a home where tears were not tolerated and were seen as a sign of weakness, and the message was always "buck up and carry on," how would you have the compassion and non-judgment that would make you a loving, supportive helper? You would not have the training to bring to the table that would enable you to create a truly helpful scenario.

Below are many areas of life experiences that would impact the perspective one would project from when trying to assist a loved one in pain. This list is by no means comprehensive, but it identifies some of the biggest culprits.

1. Family Experiences
2. Family Values
3. Societal Norms and Values
4. Cultural Expectations
5. Cultural Practices
6. Personal Beliefs
7. Personal Life Experiences
8. Personal Values
9. Peer Expectations
10. Prior Traumatic Experience

All of these factors influence who we are and what we believe and how effective or ineffective we will be with emotional communications. Without prior training and support we simply can't know the right things to say and do. We feel uncomfortable and inadequate, and that does not feel good.

The bottom-line is that "hurting people" intimidate most of us. They seem fragile, and we don't want to break them. Their situation is all too real a reminder that at any given moment we are only seconds away from feeling just as devastated and wracked with the agony of loss as they are.

When we are uncomfortable and don't know how to communicate supportively, we tend to fall back on what we learned growing up. Too often this kind of communication is based on myths and misinformation. We say unhelpful, trite things like "I guess God needed him more than you did." Or, "You just have to be strong."

These kinds of statements usually come from something we heard or were told. In the moments when we don't know what to say, the subconscious dredges them up from the dark recesses of our minds, and before we know it we are saying that dreaded wrong thing. It doesn't take too many of these experiences to teach us that communicating with someone who is emotional is a danger zone.

Because we care, we don't want them to be in pain. But ironically, more often than not, our discomfort with their pain causes us to say or do something that causes further injury.

We learn so many things in school and in the advanced training we do for our professional careers, and yet we learn very little that improves our skills as members of the human race.

My mother came from an upbringing that taught her that you don't speak up when you are upset or hurt. You don't air the family secrets in public. Even in childbirth she did not cry out because of family teachings. When she got upset with my dad she would just clam up… for long periods of time. What else could she do? She had no skills for expressing her feelings and healing the problem.

So is it any wonder that when my husband started saying and doing things that hurt and upset me, I couldn't open my mouth and tell him. I truly didn't know how to do it. I wanted to, I needed to, but when I opened my mouth… no words came out. This went on for years until I couldn't stand it anymore and finally told him I wanted a divorce. He was shocked because I had never told him that anything was wrong. This is a perfect example of how family values and experiences impact our ability to say the things we need to say to be happy, healthy, functional human beings.

Without really understanding why, we find a million reasons why we can't speak our truth or call or go visit someone in need. They all seem legitimate in the moment, but when you really get to the bottom of it, we don't have the knowledge or skills or mindset to know what to say or do, and that creates a dreaded sinking feeling each time we encounter it. No one wants the encounter with that feeling. In addition, we may also have the subconscious belief that it is weak or wrong to express feelings, and so we may subconsciously judge others who do.

Bottom-line... the reason we don't show up to help is way more about our own fears, failings and beliefs than it is about anything else. Our humanity drives us to want to help, but our beliefs, teachings and fears all too often prevent us from actually showing up.

My dream is that never again will a person in tears be left alone or be made to feel defective, wrong, selfish or any other such nonsense. Instead, I would like them to feel supported, loved unconditionally, and hopeful that, one day, the pain will end and, in the meantime, someone will be there for them to hold onto.

Humans need humans to get through the tough parts of life. Let's do what we need to do and learn what we need to learn to be able to boldly step into that helping role whenever it presents itself.

To be an effective communicator you must begin by setting the right Intention. Although it is actually simple, it sets an important tone for what we do, and it is critical that it be done right. So let's take a look at what it means to set an Intention.

Paula Shaw

SETTING INTENTION

This is actually a simple but very important process. I never do a session or have any kind of important discussion without setting an Intention as to how I want it to go. We even set an Intention before every episode of my radio show. Why? Because declaring your Intention out loud lets the energy know how you want it to show up. In a universe composed of electromagnetic energy, which Quantum Physics tells us shows up in accordance with the expectation of the observer, it is of utmost importance that we take charge and let the energy clearly know what we want to experience.

I always feel that without setting an Intention, it is as if I am casting my fate to the wind. That is not what I want. I'd much rather create the outcome I desire than accept whatever comes along.

When you are about to talk to someone in emotional pain, it is very important that you set an Intention to be present, comforting, supportive and **without judgment.** Your goal is to provide a healing, safe place for your hurting loved one, not one in which they will need to explain or defend! This defeats the whole purpose of having a heartfelt, consoling, compassionate conversation.

So please don't miss this step! Here is an example of setting an Intention for helping someone in emotional need.

"My Intention is to be present, to come from my heart and not my head and to provide unconditional love, comfort and support. My Intention is to listen, stay tuned in to what is needed in each moment and provide whatever that is to the best of my ability, letting go of my needs and my ideas about what *should* happen. I seek to serve, not control or teach."

Don't forget that as the conversation evolves, you can set mini-Intentions throughout it. This can be especially helpful in those moments when you don't know what to say. Should that happen, you might want to set an Intention like this: "My Intention is to listen and be open to guidance as to what to say and do, to truly be of help."

I can't tell you how many times when I am in session with a client and simply don't know what to say, that I fall back on an Intention like this and suddenly a thought or an insight opens up, and the conversation takes a very positive or productive turn.

Remember, you don't need to solve the problems of the person you are trying to help. Most of the time the important solutions have to come from them anyway. But that door will open more easily for them if you create safety and a loving, supportive environment through setting the right Intention.

Paula Shaw

BEING THERE

To really help a person in emotional pain, your body and your mind must be in the same place. You can't start planning the grocery list or thinking about your date last night when someone is baring their soul and expressing their pain to you. As true as your motivation to help might be, if the hurting person senses that "nobody is home," they will have no motivation to speak. Have you ever had the experience of being on the phone with somebody, opening up about something important, and suddenly you just know that they are checking their email or reading a web site? How badly did you want to go on talking?

In spite of my training, I have been guilty of this myself. Sometimes one of my children will call and I'm right in the middle of a piece I am writing or a text I am sending, and I will try to keep doing both. Knowing me well, and knowing that they

15

deserve better, my children will usually call me out on this in a friendly way and invite me to get back to them when I am truly available. But remember, an emotionally wounded person won't necessarily have that level of strength and courage.

You can't multitask when you are truly listening. This is a tough habit to break because we do it all day, every day. The biggest problem with life today is that we don't have the luxury to deal with one thought at a time. We all have too much on our proverbial plates. The problem is that if we are really going to rise above our stressed, mundane thinking, we have to be able to get calm and still and truly tune in to what is in front of us.

This may sound simple, but have you looked around lately? How often do you see a family out to dinner together that is fully engaged in conversation? More often than not, most of them are looking at their phones or some other form of digital babysitter. This may be OK when life is working pretty well, but trust me, it doesn't even come close to what is needed when someone is in need of emotional support. We have to be willing to stop being focused on Facebook and text messages, turn off the phone and look someone in the eye and truly say: "I am here for you."

Real listening comes from the heart, where sympathy and healing begin. To listen intently, the listener must be fully present in the moment. It requires practice and energy, but the effect can be amazing. When the listener puts all other thoughts aside and truly listens empathetically, the speaker's emotional floodgates may open and release long-pent-up feelings. This is the most important healing thing that could happen. As this deep listening continues, the speaker often comes up with his or her own solutions to problems. This is a tremendous gift to give to someone in pain. So **Be Present**... **Listen**... and magical, healing things will happen.

Paula Shaw

LISTENING

I begin this chapter by saying something fairly shocking for a book entitled *Saying the Right Thing*. What I am going to tell you is: **what you say doesn't really matter nearly as much as what you don't say!**

Whaaat? What are you saying? I am saying that what matters most is that you **Listen!**

People in emotional pain need to be listened to, not supplied with answers. Especially in this kind of conversation, there needs to be a balance between talking and listening. As the helper you don't need to pontificate or spout the Wisdom of the Ages. They know deep inside that there are no easy answers to the most important questions they are asking themselves, and they aren't really expecting answers from those who console them.

The Buddha said, and I am paraphrasing, "If your mouth is open, you're not learning." Steven

Covey added: "Most of us don't listen with an intent to understand, we listen with the intent to reply." This kind of listening is not helpful. Listen to learn, and be amazed that you are being allowed to be privy to this person's journey through hell.

If you truly wish to respond to the needs of those who are hurting, your consoling actions should typically begin with a distinct emphasis on listening and hearing, not talking. If you want to help someone in pain, you have to remember that the conversation isn't about you. You don't need to equate your experiences with what the person is going through, except maybe briefly to give them a sense that you really get why they are in so much pain. This is not the time to tell all the dirty details of your painful experience. Keep the focus on the person you set out to help!

Famed therapist and author M. Scott Peck said it best: "Since true listening involves a setting aside of the self, it also temporarily involves a total acceptance of the other. Sensing this acceptance, the speaker will feel less and less vulnerable and more and more inclined to open up the inner recesses of his or her mind to the listener."

There is awe-inspiring power in the silence of listening and a clear message: "I'm right here, I care, and I'm with you. I may not be sure what to say, but I'm ready to listen."

Listen without judgment, and respond with feeling words. This is critical. If you are listening to what someone says and you are in a place of judgment, they will sense it, and they will not go to deep levels of openness. Even if they don't realize it on a conscious level, they will begin to get cautious or defensive if they sense judgment. If your goal is to get them to open up and emote, you can see that a cautious, tentative feeling on the part of the speaker will never allow that kind of disclosure. Trust must be present before a person will really speak their truth and express the depths of their pain. Trust does not exist in the presence of judgment.

It is important to remember that every person is unique, so every person will have a unique way of living life, of loving, of learning and of grieving. That's why judgment or criticism completely undermines any efforts to support or console an emotionally wounded person.

We must remember that we all experience our pain at 100 percent no matter what the cause. And when we are in pain, we need room to express it in whatever way feels right. For some people this is going to mean uncontrollable sobbing; for others, anger and activity; for others, language that would make a sailor blush... and it's all OK. It's OK to express your pain in whatever way feels right. As the Listener/Helper you have to be onboard with that or you won't be helpful.

21

Paula Shaw

RESPONDING FROM THE HEART

Abandon any thoughts of needing to say something profound, poetic, inspiring or motivating. This kind of response either comes from ego or judgment. It's prioritizing your agenda rather than creating a space for a suffering person to move at their own pace, in their own way. Instead, respond from the heart with feeling words. Speak like real people speak! Say things like: "How painful." "Oh God, my heart aches for you!" "That's so awful." "How devastating!" "What confusion this must be creating for you." "It's so sad." "How scary!" "I am truly so sorry and sad for you." "What are you feeling?"

Another important concept to remember is to ask open-ended questions. For example, rather than saying "Do you feel devastated?" ask, "What are you feeling?" You don't want to set a person up for "yes" or "no" answers. That kind of response doesn't help them to open up and heal.

Even when you are present and responding with feeling words, being a good listener is difficult if your own issues of loss are unresolved. Discomfort or anxiety might arise and take you out of the moment if the speaker's conversation touches upon issues that still cause you pain.

In the best-case scenario, your own grief work would be completed, and these unresolved issues wouldn't exist. However, if this should not be the case, the best course of action would be to tell the speaker honestly what you are feeling and then try to get back to discussion of his/her situation.

Telling the truth about your discomfort is far better than being taken out of the moment and saying something inane or hurtful because you couldn't think straight and are just trying to say something. Sometimes the things people say in such moments are unfathomable, as was done in the following true story.

"A relative said to me a year after I lost my brother, grandfather, husband and then mother, 'Come on Laurie, put on your big girl pants and get out, instead of staying home with your dead husband.' Yes, someone really did say this to me one and a half years after he died."

This kind of shocking, insensitive talk goes on all the time, and it is usually said by someone who is trying to help! So please, be honest and present and quiet as you allow the hurting person to speak and release their pent-up pain.

Once you have taken time to listen, healing conversation can begin. Remember, sadness and emotional pain are emotional, not intellectual! Helpful conversations need to encourage emotional outlet. The following are some helpful suggestions with which you might start.

Paula Shaw

BE RESPECTFUL

This is the cornerstone of every productive conversation, and it is critical to a supportive, healing one. "Be respectful," is what I say to men every time they ask me how to talk to women. In a time when so many men are afraid of saying the wrong thing to women, I think this is the centerpiece of how to communicate effectively. While it is equally true that being respectful is important in every communication with another human being, it is especially true of the conversations that happen between men and women. Women need to feel safe to really be vulnerable and open to expressing their truths. More than any other factor, I believe coming from respect creates that safety.

Respect implies that one is valued and understood. It says "I don't think I am better than you." It puts each person on an equal footing, and this creates fertile soil for a truly healing conversation.

Men don't really need to be worried about what they say to women today. Just always be sure to check yourself as to whether you are coming from respect or not. If you are, you will be heard and responded to. If you are not, then open, productive conversation is impossible. It's really not all that complicated between men and women. If there is mutual respect and kind treatment, deep levels of connection and communication are possible.

Remember, women come from a long history of being disrespected by men. They were desired by them but not respected. The issues between men and women can be easily healed when respect is present.

This is equally true of any person in pain whom you are desirous of supporting. Respectful conversation is what can help and heal; it is what is needed by everyone when life presents difficult times. Through respectful communication, it becomes possible to leap to the next level of growth and evolution on this human journey.

HELPFUL THINGS TO SAY:

1. "What happened?"

2. "I'm so sorry. Was he/she ill for a long time?"

3. "I've been thinking about you and wanted to know how you were doing."

4. "This must be a confusing and incredibly complicated time."

5. "What's it like for you these days? How are you coping?"

6. "I can't imagine how painful this must be."

7. "Were you able to have any meaningful conversations with him/her before the end?"

8. "Do you feel like talking for awhile?"

9. "When did you first realize the seriousness of the situation?"

10. "I certainly can't know exactly how your pain feels, but I remember when I lost my mom..." (Remember: be brief and share—don't compare.)

11. "This can be such a lonely time. How is it going for you?"

12. "You know, one of my favorite memories of him was..."

13. "Each person's pain is unique. What kinds of things are you experiencing?"

14. "There is so much going on for you right now, and it can be so overwhelming. Want to talk about it?"

15. "I have never experienced anything exactly like this, but I remember the time…" (Briefly share how you felt to help open up the griever.)

16. "Don't worry, I'm not going to tell you that everything happens for a reason. Right now, I'm sure you just feel that this sucks."

17. "Just so you know, I am totally onboard for helping you in any way that I can—driving you somewhere, bringing you food… whatever."

18. "I'm sorry that I didn't call sooner. Quite honestly, I didn't know what to say."

19. "Whether you feel like talking or not I am here, and I'm not going anywhere."

20. "I wish I knew the perfect thing to say to make it better, but I don't. I do love you though."

THE FOLLOWING ARE NOT HELPFUL:

1. "You must get on with your life. You've been grieving long enough."

2. "I know it's tough, but you're not the first person this has happened to."

3. "Be thankful you have another child."

4. "Don't cry. Tears won't help anything."

5. "I know exactly what you're going through."

6. "We have no right to question God's will."

7. "You're young, and you have plenty of time to find another relationship."

8. "It was really a blessing. You mustn't be selfish."

9. "You're lucky you had him for so long."

10. "Don't feel guilty or ashamed... you're only human."

11. "You have to be strong. You must hold yourself together for the sake of the children."

12. "I heard you're not taking it too well."

13. "You know grief just takes time."

14. "You've got to keep yourself busy so you don't think about it."

15. "It could have been worse."

16. "It's for the best. You deserve better."

17. "God never gives a burden bigger than the back can bear. You'll be fine."

18. "I'm sorry, but we all have to go sometime."

19. "It's just a house." (Or a job or a pet or a...) "There will be another one."

20. "You have to know that God knows best. There's a reason for everything. You're going to grow through this."

While some of the above statements may be intellectually accurate, they are ineffective and possibly even abusive. Grief is an emotional state, not an intellectual one! The head isn't broken... the heart is. Emotion is the medicine of the heart. People in emotional states only feel **Heard** if they are responded to with emotion. People in pain need to relate to our humanity, not our database!

Remember, the most important ingredient in helping someone in pain is the Intention of your heart. Stay present, and stay in your Intention to comfort and support. If you do this, you will know the right things to say.

If any part of you thinks you need to get the suffering person to "snap out of it and move on," please don't act on that. Give them their space. None of us has the right to say "time's up," in regard to someone else's pain. Believe me, no one wants to be hurting any longer than they have to, but they also can't be what they are not.

In summary, there are five simple steps to successful communication:

- Set the right Intention.

- Be present.

- Comfort and support without judgment.

- Listen and allow them to speak and explore.

- Respond respectfully, from the heart, and allow the person who is hurting whatever time and process they need.

Paula Shaw

WHAT TO DO IF YOU ARE THE ONE WHO IS HURTING

Sometimes if you are the person in pain, it can be very hard to know how to tell others what you need and what you want. Too often, the one who is agonizing is worrying about being a downer to others and consequently doesn't get their own needs met. So, rather than healing, the pain keeps growing. This almost always leads to isolation, which is not conducive to healing.

I once made a huge mistake that I'm sure many of you have made as well. In my desire to cheer up my friend who had just lost a pregnancy, I didn't say anything about what had happened. Not in one single one of our conversations in any of the times that I was with her did I bring up her loss. I was there for her. I showed up and took her out and made her laugh, but I never brought up the agony she had just been through in losing the baby that she had so badly wanted.

Months later, she told me that one of the hardest parts of the loss was that she could never talk about her pain because nobody brought it up, and she didn't want to say anything and make anyone else feel bad. Oh, my lord! What an eye-opener for me. How many hurting people have we all known whom we didn't help because we didn't talk about the giant elephant that was right in the middle of their living room?

Here are some suggestions of ways to communicate to others how you feel and what you need if you are the one who is hurting.

WHAT TO SAY IF YOU ARE
THE PERSON IN PAIN:

1. "Thank you for your concern. It means a great deal to me, but I just need to be alone right now."

2. "I am really having a hard time talking, but could you just sit with me without talking?"

3. "What I really need is a hug."

4. "There really is nothing to say. It is what it is, but I appreciate your being here."

5. "Maybe God needed him, but I need him too, and it isn't comforting to hear that right now."

6. "There really don't seem to be any good answers. I'm just trying to get through one moment at a time."

7. "Quite honestly, the future looks terrifying, empty and grim. I don't know what to do."

8. "I don't expect you to say the perfect words. It just feels good that you're here."

9. "I want to be alone, and yet I don't. Could you come and just watch a movie with me?"

10. "Just taking a walk in silence would be so helpful. Would you do that with me?"

11. "I appreciate your suggestions, and when I have a little more energy I will try them."

12. "It's so hard to keep up the façade. Thank you for allowing me to be real."

13. "I don't know what I need, but it feels good that you care and are trying."

14. "Everyone has answers and suggestions, and I appreciate the efforts that are being made, but I am clear that I am going to have to find those answers for myself."

15. "If you would like to bring by some food that would be great, but I need to warn you that I am not very good company right now."

16. "I just need to feel what I'm feeling until I'm not feeling it anymore. Hopefully you understand."

17. "I hear what you're saying, but have you ever experienced anything like this?"

18. "Just to know that you're there when I'm ready to talk is a blessing."

19. "I need time to cry and feel the pain, and I'm just not ready to socialize just yet."

20. "Your love is a blessing that feels like a life raft in a sea of pain. Thank you for being there."

IS THERE A PERFECT FORMULA FOR WHAT TO SAY?

The short answer is "no." First of all, if we are being heartfelt, that is a state that is the opposite of formulaic, so of course there is no perfect formula that could apply. In every instance there are unique aspects of the experience that need to be taken into consideration. Even in two instances of child loss, there are unique aspects to consider like age, circumstances of the death, sex of the child, whether or not there are siblings, etc.

So what I am saying is, how could there be one perfect statement that works for all instances of child loss? That being said, if you keep the principles in mind that I have shared in this book—be present, listen, and let you heart lead—you will find the right thing to say. Remember what I said earlier: people who are in pain need to relate to your humanity, not your database.

I have found that when I absolutely don't know what to say, the best thing I can do is to tell the truth. I just honestly say, "I don't know what to say. My heart aches for you." Then I hug them, if it is appropriate. If I do that, I can feel comfortable that I have done the most healing thing I could do. Hurting people have highly sensitive radar for bullshit, so don't go there.

Everyone feels their pain at 100 percent, so it doesn't matter if they have been hurt by the loss of an animal, a job, a huge disappointment, a parent's words, a romance gone, or a favorite piece of jewelry missing. The loss, or change, has created emotional pain. This is the common denominator that needs to be addressed. Someone you care about is hurting, and you want to support and comfort. It's really simple. We complicate it when we get caught up in our own ego need to be wise and profound. When people are in pain, the most important thing you can be is **Real**! From the well of authenticity, compassion, love and wisdom flow naturally. When a person in emotional pain senses this, their words and feelings find a voice, and then true healing begins.

Isn't this good news? We don't have to have all the answers. We don't have to be wise or smart or trained or experienced. We just have to be there... body and heart... then just listen, supportively and compassionately.

AND A CHILD SHALL LEAD

Some of the most comforting words and deeds I have ever seen and experienced have come from children, because they have no worry about the right thing to say or do. They just do what comes naturally. They know instinctively that touch helps. They ask questions and let the sad person talk. Most importantly of all, they have no standards or expectations that they are holding anyone to. Doing that undermines safety and makes the person who is hurting feel damaged or defective.

Maybe this is the most important thing I can tell you… when you want to help someone who is hurting, let your Inner Child lead the way.

I remember my friend Hal, who lost his wife of thirty-three years, told me that one of the greatest sources of comfort at the funeral was his little granddaughter gently rubbing his hand throughout the service.

Another client, Helen, told me that one of the most helpful things for her when she lost her husband was a chat with a neighbor child on the street, who said to her, "I'm sad. I miss Buck. Can we talk about how funny he was?"

Think about how truly therapeutic that line of dialogue was. It was heartfelt, authentic and expressed feelings. It invited the widow to also express her feelings honestly. Then it afforded her the opportunity to engage in conversation about what she loved about her husband. This is the most important kind of conversation someone in this circumstance can have. The more we can express what we feel and what we are going through, the better we move through the feelings and don't get stuck in them. This kind of processing can only happen in conversation with another safe person who will listen and not try to tell us how we should be, or what we should think or do.

One of the most wonderful things about most children is that they don't check the societal norms, or a book of etiquette, before they have an emotional reaction. My daughter is a part-time nanny, and she recently texted me a great story about the honesty of children. She was sharing with the seven-year-old child she is a nanny for that she might have a date that week with a guy she met on Bumble, an online dating service. Upon hearing this, the child, without a second's hesitation, said, "Wow! You must be really desperate for love to go on that machine!"

LOL big time! Her unabandoned truth brings to mind the words of a song that talks about two of our greatest sources of comfort:

> Bless the beasts and the children;
> Give them shelter from a storm;
> Keep them safe;
> Keep them warm.
> Light their way
> When the darkness surrounds them;
> Give them love, let it shine all around them.

God bless the beasts and the children... they are completely real, and they keep us in touch with our real selves. I am so grateful for them.

Paula Shaw

WHAT WE DO CAN MATTER AS MUCH AS WHAT WE SAY

I just got off the phone with a client who faced the first holiday season without his wife of forty years.

He and his grown children were planning to gather to celebrate Christmas together, and when we first talked, he told me he had planned several different, special things so that everyone would enjoy Christmas and not feel sad.

He had bought tickets to a wonderful show and ordered unique food for Christmas dinner. Many thoughtful and wonderful plans had been laid. But I told him that while this was all great, none of it was going to change the fact that Mom, Grandma and Wife would not be there.

I suggested that in addition to the other things he'd planned, that they set a place for her at the table, with a special candle. Before the meal the candle could be passed to each person, and they could either hold it in silence, thinking about her, or they could share a memory of her.

I was delighted to hear that they did do this, and he said it went beautifully and was really one of the most wonderful, authentic parts of their Christmas celebration.

It does not help us to heal if we pretend that something tragic didn't happen. We need to have the courage to face the truth, feel it and talk about it.

I remember, years ago, hearing that a big star of stage and screen had died in February, and the family announced that they would be gathering to commemorate her life later in the summer at a more *convenient* time.

My friends... death, loss and emotional turmoil aren't convenient! But they are part of life. We need to acknowledge them and deal with them in the moment that they happen. If we don't, we have to push the pain away, and that saps our energy and causes physical and emotional complications.

I was recently in a session with a client, whom I will call Noreen. I asked her how her holidays had been, and she enthusiastically said, "Oh they were fine." Now, I knew that she and her son had been estranged for at least three years, so I asked the dangerous question, "Did you hear from your son?"

"No," she replied, "but I didn't expect to, and I'm fine."

"OK," I said. "So you're sure you're OK?"

"Absolutely!" she emphatically responded.

"So how can I help you tonight? What would you like to be better or different?"

"I'd like to be able to walk without pain!" she heartily replied.

At that point, I inquired about what was preventing her from walking easily and found out that lower back pain, referring down her leg, was the culprit. In looking at the problem beneath the problem, which is what I do, I saw that the problem area was in the region of the Root Energetic Center and the Sacral Energetic Center. These two energy centers are about relationships and connection to family.

What is my point? Even though her conscious mind was convinced that she had handled not hearing from her son on one more Christmas, while still not knowing why he withdrew, her body and heart had registered the emotional pain that her mind wouldn't let in. This had resulted in a physical condition. How do you think cancer is created? Why does one person get the flu and another in the presence of it, day after day, gets nothing?

We are whole beings. The heart and the mind don't operate independently of the body.

Do your best to deal with your pain in the moment that you feel it. Process it, and let it move through.

I share with you an example of this from my own life. As I was writing this, I was googling the words to "Bless the Beasts and the Children." Even though I was in masculine, linear thinking "Go Mode" when I heard the music of the song, I started to sob and feel the pain of all the losses I had endured since I first heard this song.

As YouTube is wont to do, a moment later I heard another Carpenters song, "We've Only Just Begun," and I thought about my first marriage where this song was sung at the wedding, and out of the blue I started to sob again. This was totally unexpected… it was crazy!

But, to my credit, knowing what I know and am now sharing with you, I let it roll. I sobbed, I wailed, I let it flow. And you know what? Now I'm capable of being able to share it with you.

I'm present because I moved the emotion through my body. I didn't push it down or put it away to deal with another day. I felt it right here, right now and let it go. This is actually how the emotional system was designed to work. Feelings are supposed to arise and move through your being, be expressed, then move up and out. When we allow this natural pathway, everything works. It's when we push or set aside our feelings for "**a more convenient time**" that we create problems.

LIFE IS IN SESSION... LET'S HOLD HANDS AS WE CROSS THE STREET

Even though Madison Avenue seems to want us all to think that if we do the right things, own the right things, wear the right things, and drive the right things we will be happy, I think most of us are pretty clear that this isn't true.

In fact, just recently I heard my friend Shirlene say that she'd reached the place in life where she wanted to get rid of a lot of the stuff she had accrued over the years. And strangely enough, in the moment that this realization hit her, she was also struck by the reality of what she'd sacrificed and gone through to get it all in the first place.

We're all on this journey of life, and it is often very confusing because we are mostly taught to devalue and push aside anything that isn't bliss or the version of happiness dictated by advertising industry standards. And yet, don't we always learn the most from the painful experiences we endure? Isn't it true that we grow most when we are figuring out how to solve a problem or fix something that isn't working?

Yet, we think if we didn't get the affluent, well-provided-for upbringing with a wise, powerful father and a loving, devoted mother, that we have been ripped off of our birthright to live the fairy-tale American dream.

The truth is, none of us have ideal circumstances all of the time. And that isn't necessarily a bad thing if we use those experiences to grow wiser and kinder.

* * *

I've always loved the story that Joan Boresynko, Ph.D., tells about her mother, with whom she had endured a life-long contentious relationship, plagued with disappointment, criticism and difficulty. It wasn't until the moment of her mother's death, when the hospital room filled with light, that she suddenly realized that her mother had been the person who had given her the most in life and who had actually helped her the most. This was because her mom had provided the resistance against which Joan had to push in order to become whom she was meant to be!

Life is not without difficulties and challenges for any of us, but those difficulties provide opportunities to experience love and growth and comfort with others. The details of what we say and do never matter as much as our intentions to love, comfort and support. I think this has been true since the dawn of time. We feel, we hurt, and we take care of each other. Nothing matters more in the big picture.

Think back on your life. What stands out most? Is it what you accrued or what you felt and experienced, especially in the moments when you were feeling sad, scared and alone? Who was there? Who said something that changed your whole perspective? Who did something that gave you hope?

No matter what economic status we have, what level of education or material gain we have achieved, love, comfort and support are always experiences we can offer each other. And I submit that they are the experiences that will always matter most.

SO, WHEN SOMEONE YOU CARE ABOUT IS HURTING...

It is my hope that what I have shared with you will become part of your life and your communication style. Keep this little book close it will be a big help. Relationships are everything in life. Whether they are the relationships with colleagues, family or friends...they are what gives life meaning and joy.

Let's all commit to taking good care of the relationships that matter by having conversations that matter. As you have seen in this simple little book, being a good communicator doesn't have to be complicated. All that is required is caring enough to implement the following steps.

THE 5 STEPS OF HELPFUL, EFFECTIVE COMMUNICATION:

1. Set the Right Intention.
2. Be Present.
3. Come from a Mindset of Comfort and Support without Judgement.
4. Listen with the intent to hear, not the intent to respond.
5. Respond, when it's appropriate, from the Heart not the Head.

And always remember... Come from **Love**, and be **Authentic**. Follow your **Heart**... it knows the way.

ABOUT THE AUTHOR

 Paula Shaw CADC, DCEP, is a Life Transitions Expert, an innovator, visionary and pioneer in the field of Energy Psychology. She is also a best-selling author, keynote speaker and host of Change It Up Radio.

For more than twenty-five years, Paula has been passionate about guiding and supporting those who are navigating the upheaval, stress and trauma of Change and Challenge.

By combining elements of traditional therapy with cutting edge Energy Psychology tools, Paula has helped thousands to transition from pain to peace, getting relief from stress, grief, depression and anxiety. She also helps her clients to identify and clear blocks to success, eliminate relationship issues, overcome their fears and shift self-sabotaging patterns and feelings to achieve confidence and inner peace.

She is the author of the life-changing books, *Chakras: The Magnificent Seven* and *Grief... When Will This Pain Ever End?*

She has earned degrees in Education and Communications from Long Beach State University, with graduate work at Loyola Marymount University, where she advanced her studies to become a Certified Alcohol and Drug Abuse Specialist and a Certified

Grief Specialist. Grief has become a central focus of her work, as it is often a core issue in addictive and dysfunctional behavior.

KEYNOTE TOPICS:

What Do I Say to My People in Emotional Pain?

As a leader, do you know what to say to the person on your team who is struggling with serious emotional pain? Finding the right words to say when someone is hurting—from a death, divorce, loss, or other life challenge—can be uncomfortable and frustrating. No one wants to unintentionally hurt someone who is already suffering, but until now it's been hard to know what to do.

Paula provides a clear understanding of what to say and what NOT to say to people in emotional pain. She gives you the perfect words and the right spirit in which to convey them, and she coaches you on how to apply a step-by-step approach to communicating compassionately with those who are going through major life transitions.

Mastering the Stress of Change and Challenge

Is your need for internal change creating frustration, anger, or apathy within your team?

Life is uncertain and stressful changes that knock us off balance are a part of life. During this experiential presentation, Paula offers effective, innovative tools that calm the body and mind to help participants eliminate stress, overcome challenges, and embrace change. These scientifically proven tools and strategies are drawn from Quantum Physics and Energy Psychology and have helped thousands of people achieve balance and inner peace. Paula shows you how to shift and maintain your energetic state anytime, anywhere... even during periods of stress, loss, or uncertainty.

Eliminate Beliefs and Behaviors that Sabotage Productivity!

In this interactive presentation, Paula coaches participants who are experiencing stress, apathy, negativity and a lack of productivity to rebalance their energies and regain a creative, collaborative, productive mindset. She uses mind/body tools and techniques from the fields of Quantum Physics and Energy Psychology to identify and remove the subconscious limiting beliefs that underlie unproductive behaviors. These techniques can be implemented by your team quickly and easily to create dynamic results that transform the working environment.

CONTACT PAULA SHAW

Web Site: PaulaShaw.com

Email: Pshawlight@gmail.com

Phone: (858) 480-9234

Facebook: Paula Shaw, Paula Shaw Counseling,
Change It Up Radio, Bridges Podcast

Instagram: ChangeItUpRadio

YouTube.com: Paula Shaw Counseling, Change It Up Radio

Twitter: @PaulaShawcoach

LinkedIn: Paula ShawChangeitupradio

Made in the USA
San Bernardino, CA
21 November 2018